WORKING IS A LOUSY WAY TO EARN A LIVING

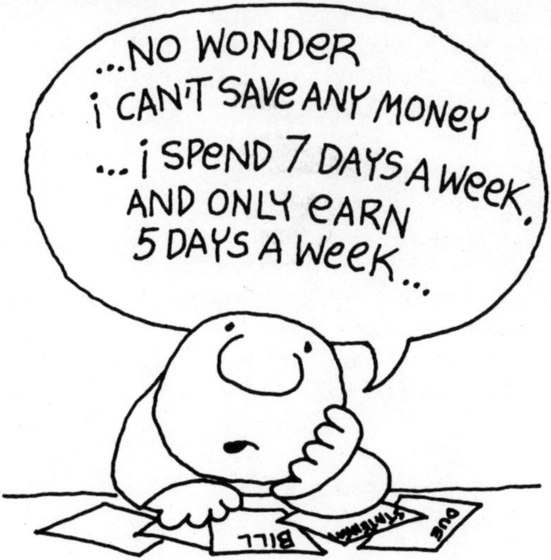

...NO WONDER
i CAN'T SAVE ANY MONEY
...i SPEND 7 DAYS A WEEK,
AND ONLY EARN
5 DAYS A WEEK...

Andrews and McMeel, Inc.

A Universal Press Syndicate Company

Kansas City • New York • Washington

ZIGGY™ is syndicated internationally by Universal Press Syndicate

 For information write Andrews and McMeel, Inc., a Universal Press Syndicate Company, 4400 Johnson Drive, Fairway, Kansas 66205.

ISBN: 0-8362-1970-8
Library of Congress Catalog Card Number: 81- 65624

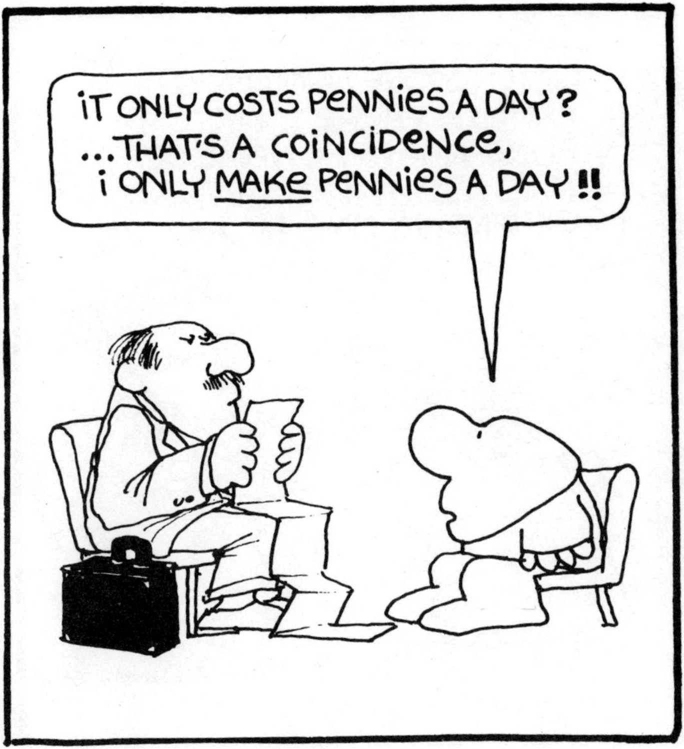
IT ONLY COSTS PENNIES A DAY? ...THAT'S A COINCIDENCE, I ONLY MAKE PENNIES A DAY!!

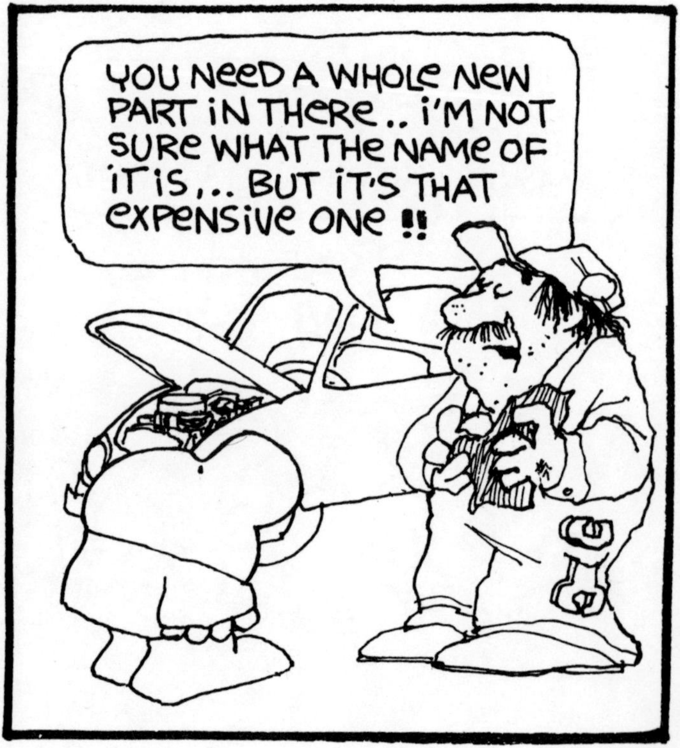
YOU NEED A WHOLE NEW PART IN THERE .. I'M NOT SURE WHAT THE NAME OF IT IS,.. BUT IT'S THAT EXPENSIVE ONE !!

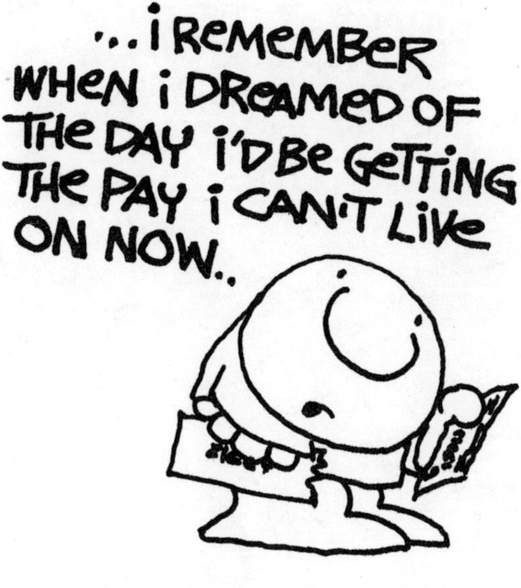
...i REMEMBER WHEN i DREAMED OF THE DAY i'D BE GETTING THE PAY i CAN'T LIVE ON NOW..

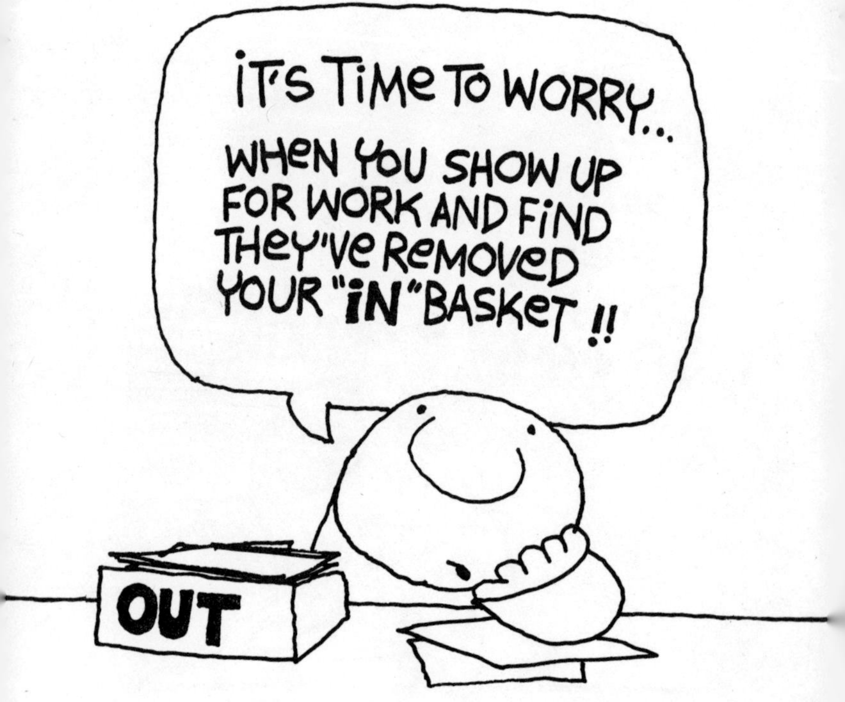
IT'S TIME TO WORRY...
WHEN YOU SHOW UP FOR WORK AND FIND THEY'VE REMOVED YOUR "IN" BASKET !!
OUT

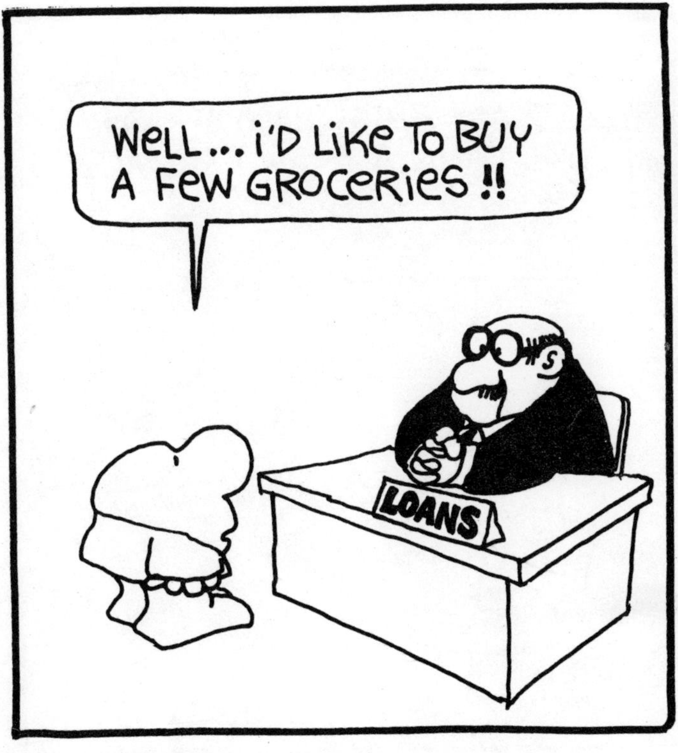
WELL... I'D LIKE TO BUY A FEW GROCERIES !!
LOANS

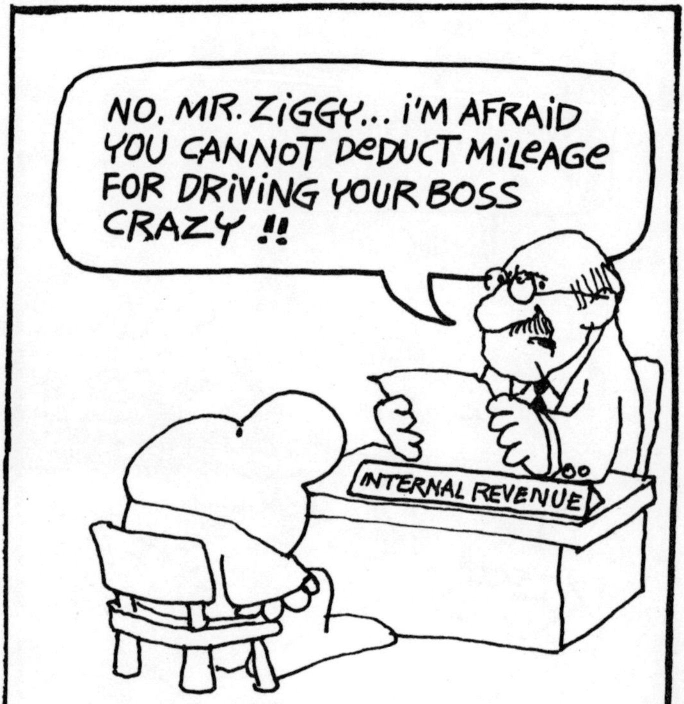
NO, MR. ZIGGY... I'M AFRAID YOU CANNOT DEDUCT MILEAGE FOR DRIVING YOUR BOSS CRAZY !!
INTERNAL REVENUE

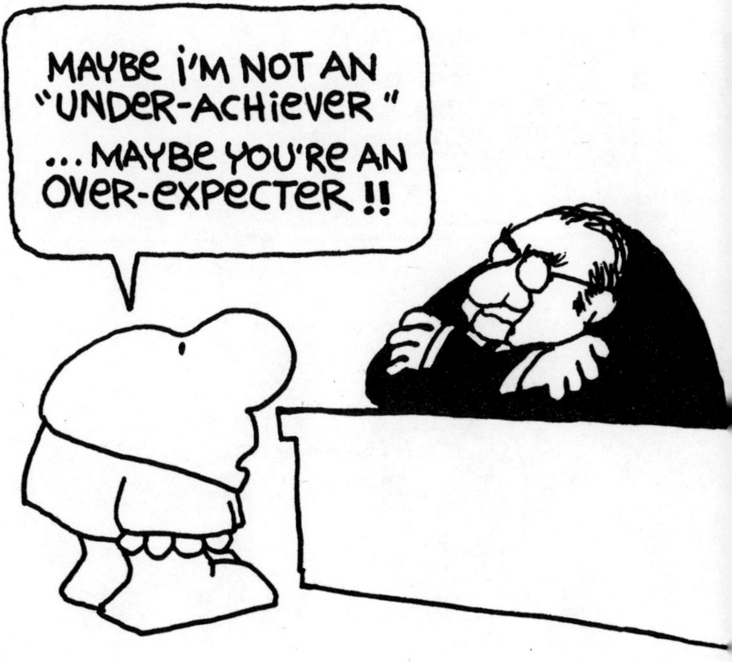
MAYBE i'M NOT AN "UNDER-ACHiEVER" ...MAYBE YOU'RE AN OVER-EXPECTER !!

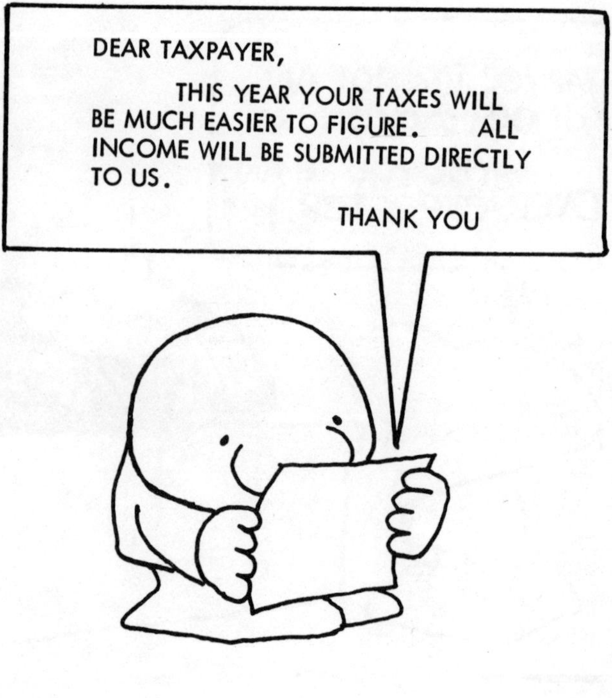
DEAR TAXPAYER,
THIS YEAR YOUR TAXES WILL BE MUCH EASIER TO FIGURE. ALL INCOME WILL BE SUBMITTED DIRECTLY TO US.
THANK YOU

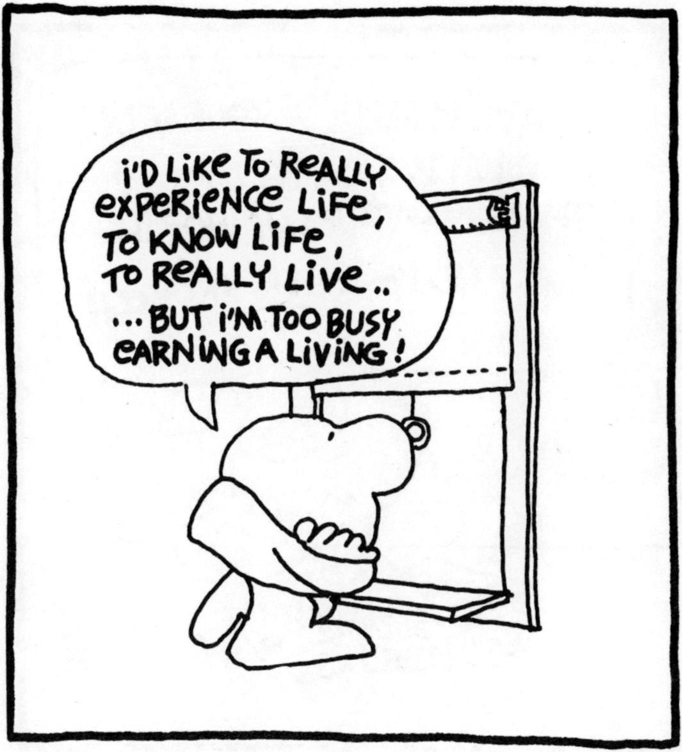
I'D LIKE TO REALLY EXPERIENCE LIFE, TO KNOW LIFE, TO REALLY LIVE.. ...BUT I'M TOO BUSY EARNING A LIVING!

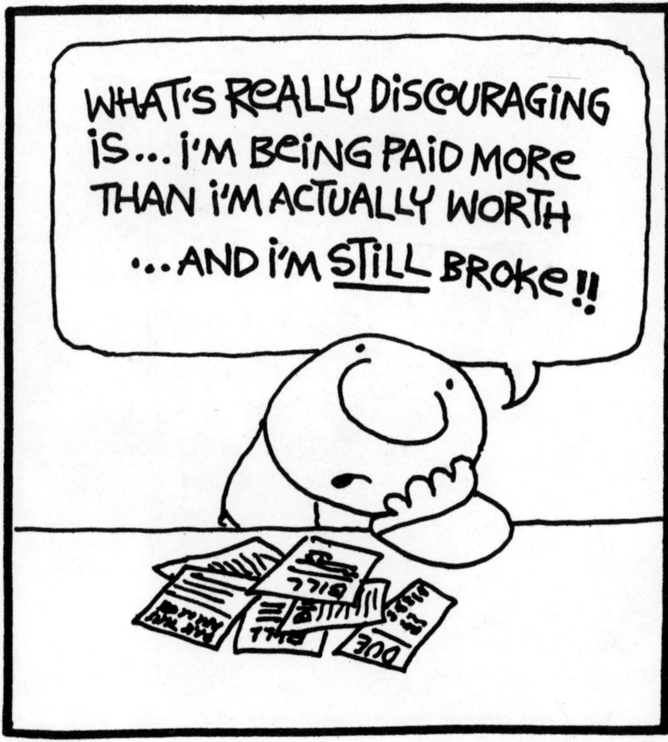
WHAT'S REALLY DISCOURAGING IS... I'M BEING PAID MORE THAN I'M ACTUALLY WORTH ...AND I'M STILL BROKE!!

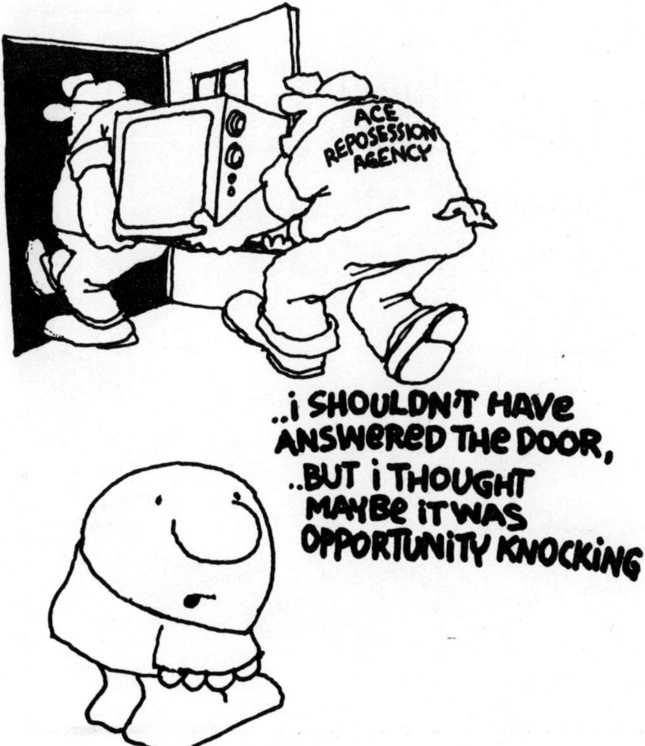
ACE
REPOSESSION
AGENCY
..i SHOULDN'T HAVE ANSWERED THE DOOR,
..BUT i THOUGHT MAYBE iT WAS OPPORTUNiTY KNOCKiNG

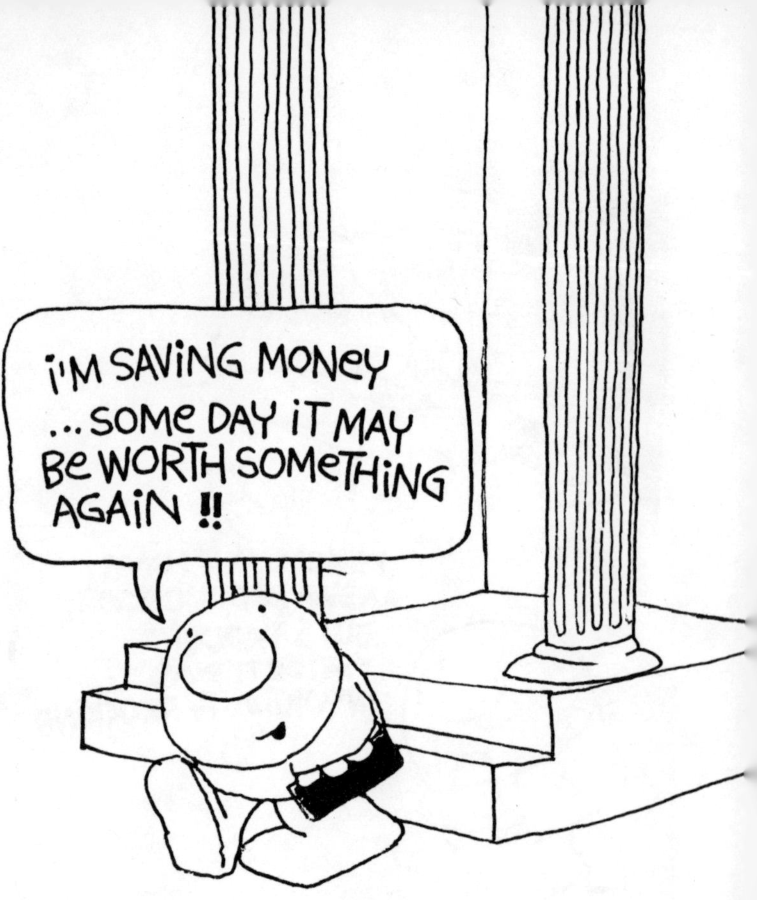
I'M SAVING MONEY ...SOME DAY IT MAY BE WORTH SOMETHING AGAIN !!

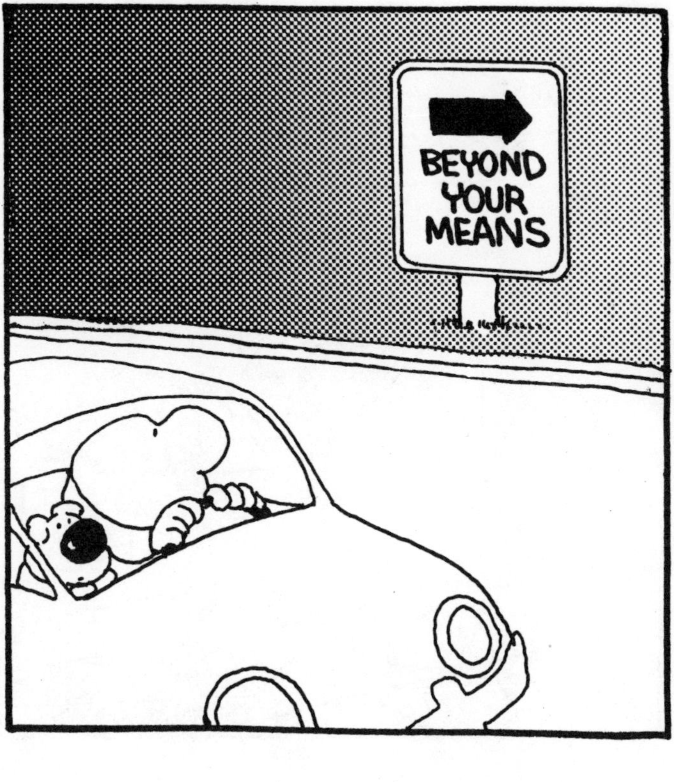
BEYOND YOUR MEANS

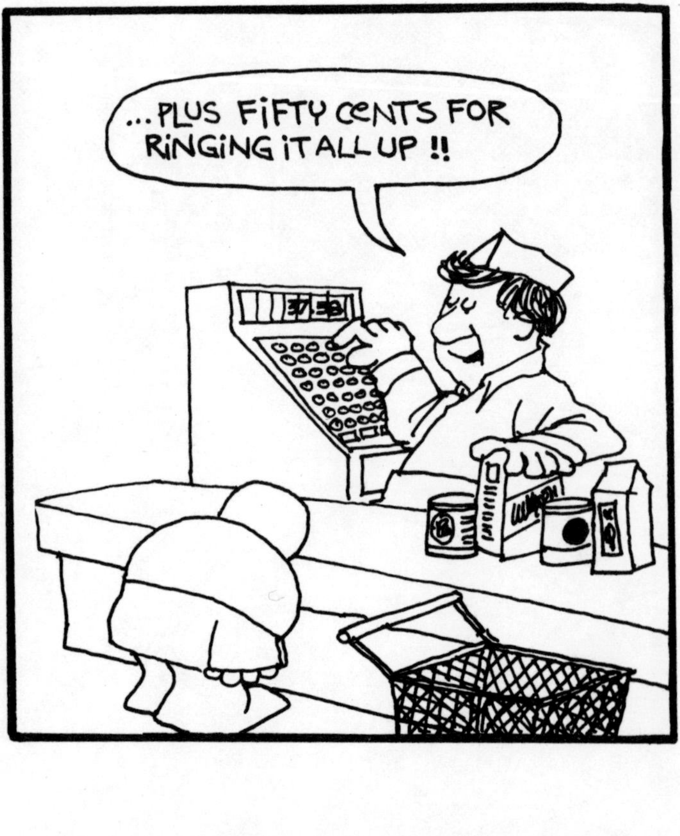
...PLUS FIFTY CENTS FOR RINGING IT ALL UP !!

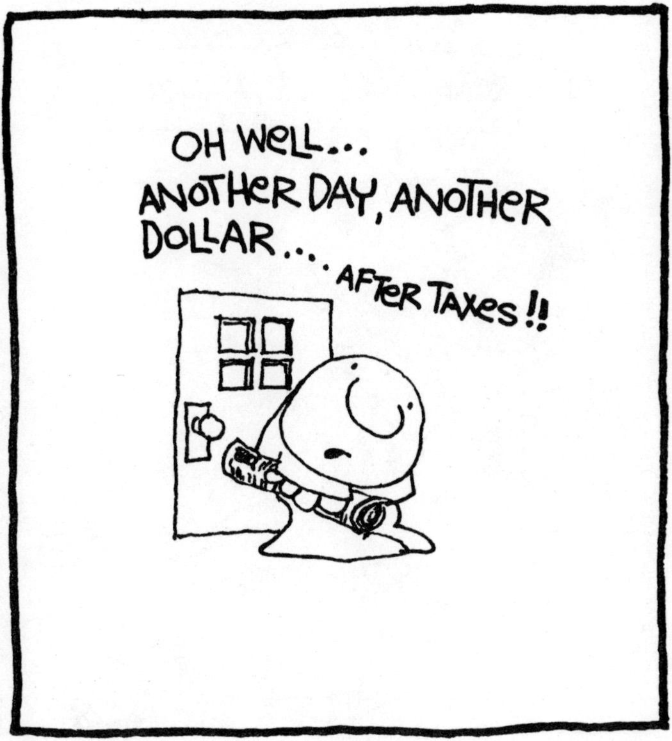
OH WELL...
ANOTHER DAY, ANOTHER DOLLAR.... AFTER TAXES!!

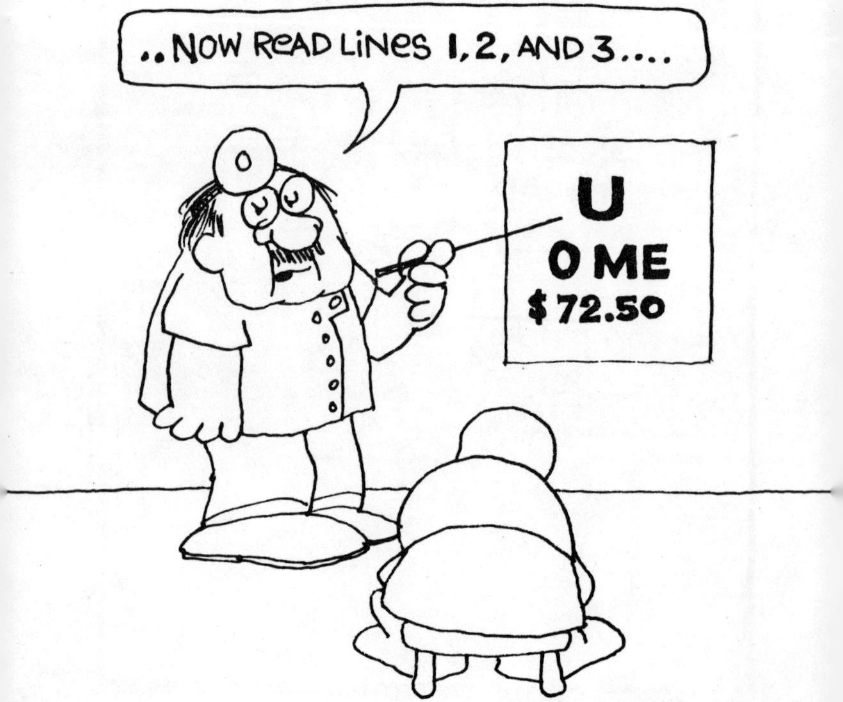
..NOW READ LINES 1, 2, AND 3....
U
O ME
$ 72.50

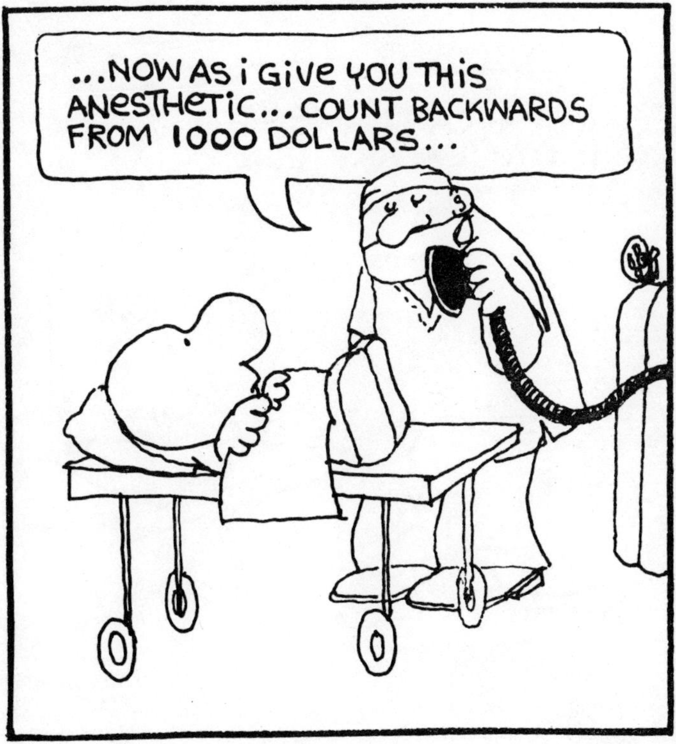
...NOW AS i GiVe YOU THiS ANeSTHeTiC..., COUNT BACKWARDS FROM 1000 DOLLARS...

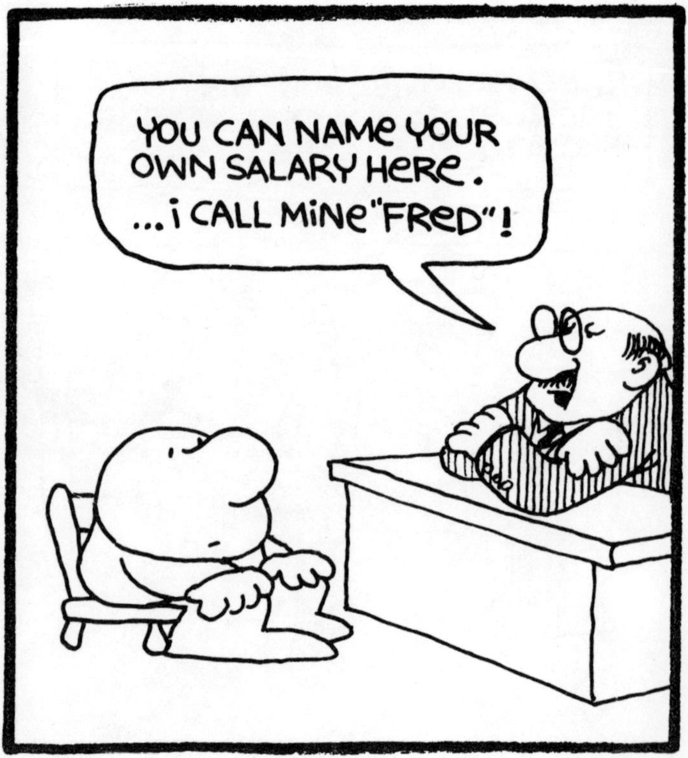
YOU CAN NAME YOUR OWN SALARY HERE. ...I CALL MINE "FRED"!

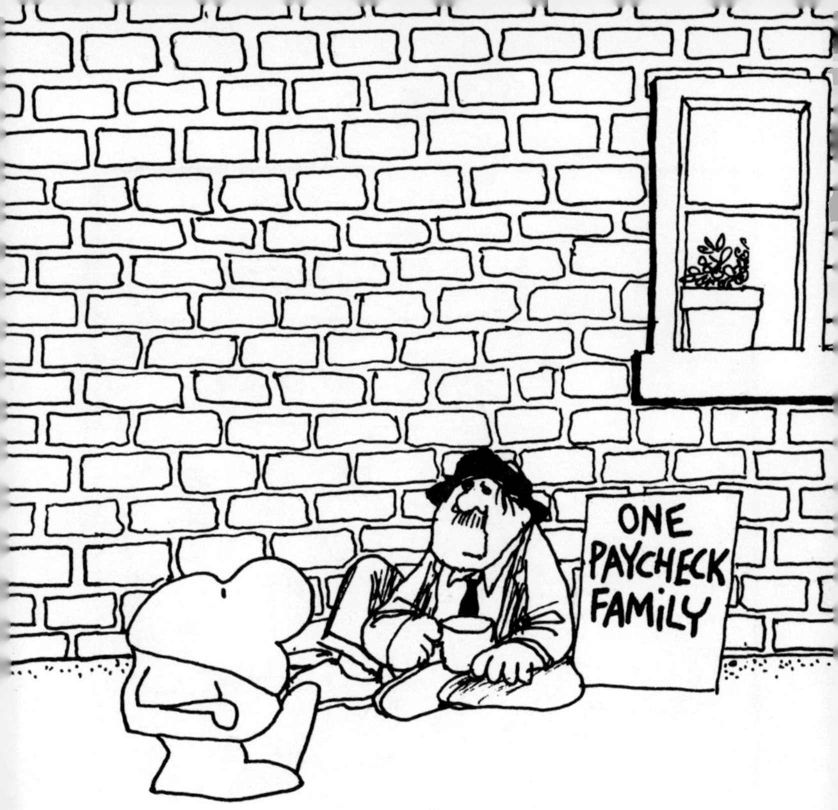
ONE
PAYCHECK
FAMILY

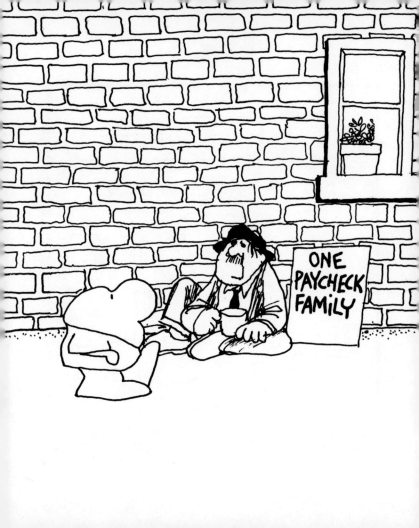

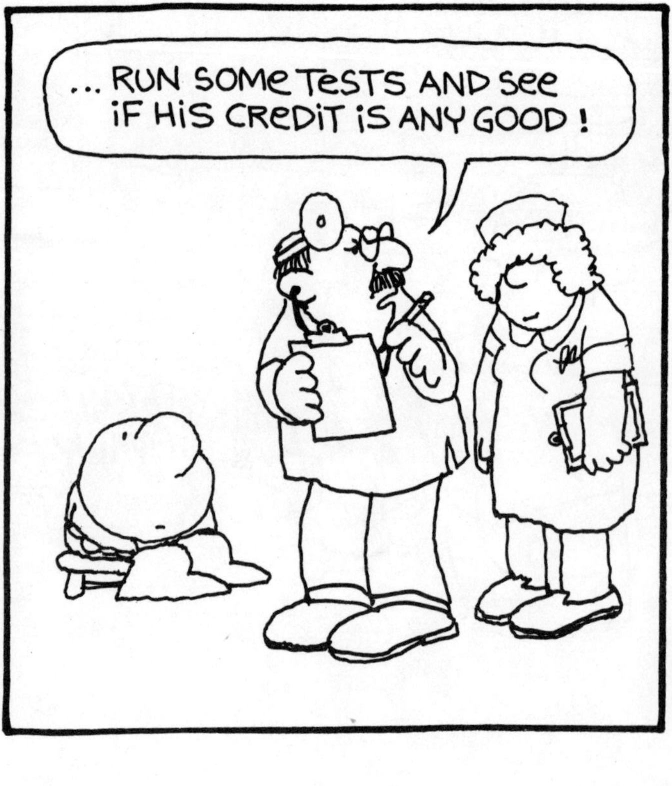
... RUN SOME TESTS AND SEE IF HIS CREDIT IS ANY GOOD!

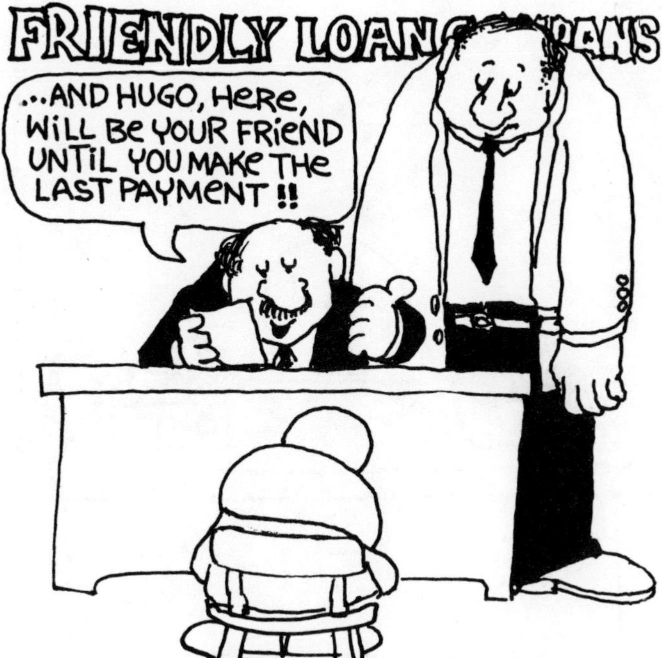
FRIENDLY LOAN
...AND HUGO, HERE, WILL BE YOUR FRIEND UNTIL YOU MAKE THE LAST PAYMENT !!

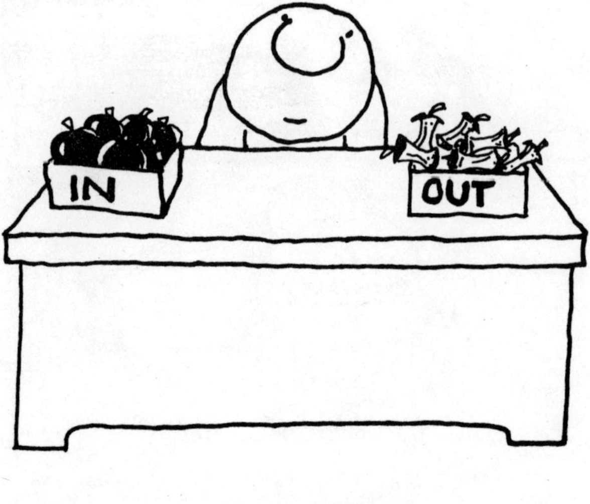
IN
OUT